LARRY GREEN

First, I would like to thank God my Father and my Lord and Savior Jesus Christ. I honor them because of the direction my life has taken, and the mercy and Love shown to me throughout this entire ordeal. Also, my lovely wife Saundra who encouraged and stood by me every step of the way while writing this book. I thank my loving mother and Grand Mother, the late

Mrs. Carrie M. Green and, Mrs. Carrie L. Green Wooten.

May they both rest in peace!

TABLE OF CONTENTS

CHAPTER ONE

INTRODUCTION

I grew up in a small southeastern town where God, family, and hard work were the keys to success and prosperity. No longer a small town, it still holds true in most cases that God, family, and hard work are still the keys to success and prosperity. There have been so many changes in the past couple of generations; it's a miracle that these principles have survived at the center of such a suburban community. In my quest to find the real secret for the survival of these principles, it seemed to defy any stretch of the imagination that God and family are still important. During my quest, I found that in the city of Wilmington, North Carolina, there seem to be enough churches to put one on every corner and that number is steadily growing. Believe me, there are a lot of corners in my hometown. This led me to ask myself if there are so many churches in this city, then why isn't this city more like heaven on earth? Somewhere in time, it seems that we (the Church) have lost sight of our purpose and our mission here on earth. I have observed that the church today hardly resembles the early church. Surely there are those who may question this or even argue this theory but the fact remains, it seems we have lost sight of our true vision not to mention our virtue. Nevertheless, we are the church, the object of Gods' unmatchable love, the hope for a dying world. Strangely enough I have found that instead of working to help establish the Kingdom of God, there are those who are constantly building their own kingdoms right here on earth. It seems that we are either trying to expand, build or establish more and more churches, not in the name of the Lord, but in the name of the pastors, bishops or those members who gave or are giving the most financial support. It seems that instead of Christ, things, prestige, or status is the center or reason for our worship. What has happened? First, we look to the Word of God and the Holy Spirit, THE POWER, FOR CHRISTIAN LIVING THE MORE ABUNDANT LIFE. Without this power, we have nothing, nor can we do what we are commanded to do. I have found that some would dare try to live this life without this power. I should know because I have tried. And each time I found myself right back where I started with nothing to show but testimonies of disappointments. At each point of failure there was a process of learning taking place that I was not aware of at the time.

Nevertheless, those stumbling blocks would soon prove to be steppingstones to higher heights and deeper debt of who God is and His plan for my life. 1 don't claim to have arrived on my journey, but I know that pressing toward the mark gives me renewed strength and a deeper desire to realize God's purpose for my life. Disappointments are where I got my start. I have found that they are not always a bad thing, but they are necessary. They taught me the difference between real success and failure and what it is to have real power for all those who want to please God in the lives that they live for Him. Not knowing that I needed this power left me at a terrible disadvantage. It was always like wanting to be in the daylight without having to experience what the darkness was like first. We all have our paths to travel, some necessary and some unnecessary, but wherever the path leads, 1 think it is important to know that it leads to Life, and Life more abundant.

CHAPTER TWO
THERE MUST BE A CHANGE

Change is inevitable, it will take place whether we want it to or not. All of God's creation, from the sun water, and the planets which include our earth changes on a regular basis. Even the 37.2 trillion cells in the human body are totally replenished every seven years. Everything must and somehow does change. Growth itself is somehow miraculously perpetuated through change. In other words, without change, there can be no growth. There is an old saying, "It's a bad wind that doesn't change". Everything must change, and if it does not then something must be wrong. When I was a young boy growing up in Wilmington, North Carolina, both in the city and mostly in the country on a farm, living with my grandparents and cousins, I got to see the best and worst of both worlds. With it, I learned a lot of good lessons and bad habits. While living in the country, we, including myself and sometimes nine other cousins not including our grandparents, all had our share of work to do on that farm. My grandparents, who we all called mamma and daddy, were sharecroppers and all of us had to do our part to keep things going during the summer and the winter. One thing I used to like to do in my spare time was to catch tadpoles and place them into one of my grandmother's mason jars. I would poke a few holes in the top of the lids with the same water I caught them from, either the creek down the road or the ditch out in front of the house. Every day I would be excited when getting off the bus from school. I would rush in before I did anything else and feed my little tadpoles and watch them swim around in that old jar. I would feed them either breadcrumbs saved from supper the night before or a little cornmeal I would sneak from the meal and flour cabinet in the kitchen. I would repeat this ritual every day until one day I noticed something strange taking place. This was the first time I had watched these tadpoles mature or go through their period of metamorphosis. I couldn't quite put my finger on it but for the first time something was happening that I was not quite familiar with. I noticed some strange changes taking place. First their eyes began to bulge as if they were about to pop out of their little heads. Each day they were getting bigger and bigger. For a while I thought I was doing something wrong, so I took the top off the jar thinking maybe they were not getting enough air. Maybe I was not changing the water often enough, so I began to change the water more often. After all of that, still more changes were taking place. Their little bodies that were very small had begun to get larger and rounder and on top of that, they began to grow legs in the rear and the front of their torsos, on either side of the tail that now seemed to be getting shorter and shorter. Sure enough, something was happening, but I had no idea what. Rather than being excited when I got off the school bus, I was worried and very concerned about what was happening to my little friends in the jar. Soon they no longer resemble tadpoles at all. What have I done? I thought. No longer was I gazing at a jar of tadpoles, but a jar full of frogs. How could this be, I asked myself. Now, with the lid off the jar, I found it increasingly difficult to contain those little fellows in the jar. Every day I had to look around for frogs that had escaped from the confines of the jar. You see, those frogs were teaching me that once a change had taken place, once they had metamorphosed, they were no longer the same. I learned that something on the inside had taken place that brought about a change on the outside of these little fellows. This is where I learned that frogs spend a lot of time in the water, but they can't live in the water as they did as tadpoles. And when I tried to force them to do so, I started coming home to dead frogs that were not able to make it out of that mess. I found the reason why so many of us are not productive after the changes have taken place in our lives is because we are still trying to stay in the jar, (the mess) and God has a greater purposed for us when we come out. Some of us are like those frogs which have gone through their period of metamorphosis but are still trying to live like tadpoles in the very mess God has given us power to come out of. In all our lives a lot of changes have taken place. With those changes a lot of growth has taken place also. No matter what form it takes, growth will always facilitate change, it makes it possible. Each of us are known by God and are destined through change to be what he has called us to be and to grow to be more complete in Him. My argument today is that change is necessary for this growth and until we the church realize who and what we truly are, and embrace the changes that have taken place, we can do no spiritual exploits for God who created us not only in His image, but in His likeness also. Change is necessary for growth, for without change, there can be no growth. It is human nature to resist change because we are afraid of the unknown. We would rather resist and fight against it tooth and nail. We become comfortable right where we are and without realizing it, we become complacent and stagnated, thinking everything is ok. This is a matter of the heart and until we deal with these heart problems, we will continue to be the church that does not resemble the early church. The early church was strong, vibrant, and full of Power for Christian Living

David, despite all he had accomplished through the Lord, found one day that he had a heart problem. So, he called on the Lord and said to him in Psalms 51 •. [9]Hide thy face from my sins and blot out all mine iniquities. [10]Create in me a clean heart, O God; and renew a right spirit within me. Let us be reminded that there is always something we must do to facilitate change in our lives.

The Holy Bible : King James Version. electronic ed. of the 1769 edition of the 1611 Authorized Version. Bellingham WA : Logos Research Systems, Inc., 1995, S. Ps 51:9-10

CHAPTER THREE
WHERE ARE YOU WALKING?

There is a lot to be said about how Christians should walk or behave in their lives. Concerning resistance to change, the Duke of Cambridge is reported to have said, "Any change at any time for any reason is to be deplored. This is the attitude that causes us to miss God and His will concerning us, his children. We have found that when a tadpole makes the transition from a tadpole to that of a frog, not only does it change in appearance but in character as well. Tadpoles cannot function as frogs and frogs certainly cannot function as tadpoles. It would be fatal for it to attempt such a thing. Everything changes once the transition takes place. Concerning the church, the apostle Paul tells us in II Corinthians 5: Therefore, if anyone be in Christ, he is a new creation. Old things have disappeared, and—look, all things have become new. This change is never with observation, meaning that it is a subtle change that takes place whether we see, or feel anything or not. God himself performs this Spiritual operation that takes place in our

Illustrations for Biblical Preaching; Edited by Michael P. Green, fonvarded by Haddon W. Robinson; copyright 1982, 1985, 1989 by Michael P.*Green.*

4 International Standard Version New Testament : Version 1.1. Print on Demand ed. Yorba Linda, CA : The Learning Foundation, 2000, S. 2 co 5:17

hearts (the very spirit of man). Once the work has begun, at this point, God has done all He is going to do concerning His plan for our salvation, the redemption of our souls, and the rest is now up to us. The apostle Paul said, "if any man be in Christ, he IS a NEW creature". By faith we must accept the fact that God has done a new thing in our lives. We may look the same, and in many cases, we may feel the same, but something NEW has happened. If God said it, must be true. We must take Him at his word. As it was with the tadpoles, what had taken place on the inside was now making a difference on the outside. Changes were taking place that not only changed the way they looked, thought, and acted but also everything they did from that moment on. We must allow the Holy Spirit to help perfect that work that has already begun. Our first objective is to realize "Where Are We Walking"? Where we walk ultimately determines where we go, it determines our destiny. The road we travel says a lot about where we end up. There are questions that must be answered concerning this change and one of them is: What did The Word of God Mean When It Said? ("BEHOLD ALL THINGS ARE BECOME NEW). When God deals with us it is always on a spiritual level. We have walked (lived) in the flesh for so long that we have lost sight of what it means to walk in the Spirit. When choosing a king for the children of Israel, the Lord spoke to Samuel the prophet in I Samuel 16: [7] But the LORD said unto Samuel, "Look not on his countenance, or on the height of his stature; because I have refused him: for the LORD seeth not as man seeth; for man looketh on the outward appearance, but the LORD looketh on the heart". Our entire existence is so attuned to the flesh, the outward appearance, what we see, and what we feel, so much so that it is all we have come to know. We have what I call is the "The Thomas syndrome'.

St. John 20:5 says, "The other disciples therefore said unto him, we have seen the Lord. But he said unto them, except I shall see in his hands the print of the nails and put my finger into the print of the nails, and thrust my hand into his side, I will not believe". We are so much like Thomas; we won't believe unless we see or feel it. Proverbs 3: 5 says: "Trust in the LORD with all thine heart and lean not unto thine own understanding. In all thy ways acknowledge him, and he shall direct thy paths". Trusting in the Lord with all our hearts by no means is it an easy task. But thank God, we can do it. We know this because he beckons us to do so. The God we serve is a just God who will never tell us to do something he knows we can't do. So again, if God said it, it must be so. We must trust God about what he says and change the way we think, what we say, and believe concerning what the word of God says about us. Again, we go to the word, Ephesians 4:22 and it says: "That ye put off concerning the former conversation the old man, which is corrupt according to the deceitful lusts; 23, And be renewed in the spirit of your mind; 24And that ye put on the new man, which after God is created in righteousness and true holiness" . The former conversation of the old man refers to the old ways of life, or our former life, which is corrupt according to the deceitful lusts, and be RENEWED in the spirit of the mind. We must begin to change the way we think by renewing our minds and not leaning to our own understanding. If not our own, then whose understanding should we lean to? I'm convinced that the word of God is the mind of God revealed to us by his Spirit of God and it is only through the word of God that our minds are renewed in Him. Our objective is to be more like Christ in all that we do. His word is his will, and his will is revealed to us by his spirit. This means that we must put on the mind of Christ (the capacity for spiritual truth, the higher powers of the soul, the faculty of perceiving divine things, of recognizing goodness and of hating evil , and say what his word says concerning all things, especially us. Now, let us focus on a few more examples of just who he (Christ)is. St John 1:1-4 says, "We proclaim to you the one who existed from the beginning, whom we have heard and seen. We saw him with our own eyes and touched him with our own hands. He is the Word of life. 2 This one who is life itself was revealed to us, and we have seen him. And now we testify and proclaim to you that he is the one who is eternal life. He was with the Father, and then he was revealed to us. We proclaim to you what we ourselves have actually seen and heard so that you may have fellowship with us. And our fellowship is with the Father and with his Son, Jesus Christ. 4We are writing these things so that you

may fully share our joy". A second example in St. John 10:27-30 says, '
'My sheep hear my voice, and I know them, and they follow me: [28] And
I give unto them eternal life, and they shall never perish, neither shall
any man pluck them out of my hand. [29] My Father, which gave them me,
is greater than all; and no man is able to pluck them out of my Father's
hand. [30] I and my father are one". The word of God is the mind of Christ
and when we began to think and do his word, then, we put on the mind
of the Lord Jesus Christ, that he may instruct us in all things concerning
righteousness. The potential of all the divine power there is, dwells in
us. If we will begin to believe what the Bible says and begin to confess
what God's word says concerning us, then He will rise up in us and give
illumination to our minds and

James Strong, The Exhaustive Concordance ofthe Bible : Showing Every Word ofthe Text ofthe
Common English Version ofthe Canonical

Books, and Every Occurrence of Each Word in Regular Order., electronic ed. (Ontario: Woodside
Bible Fellowship., 1996), G3563.

direction to our spirits, health to our bodies, and He will help us
in every aspect of life. I'm convinced that the word of God addresses
every situation in life and when we are confronted with any situation, no
matter what, we can always go to the word for instruction for whatever
we face. And when we lean to Gods' understanding, (His Word), and
take His advice concerning the situations, we-will-come-through-
blessed. Be it known, when we lean, we must lean with all, not just some
of our hearts. There may be some things we may think we are well able
to handle on our own, but it is at that time we must trust in Him with
all our hearts, not some, but all and lean not to our own understanding.
Proverbs 3:6 says, "In all thy ways acknowledge him, and he shall direct
thy paths". The question at this point is: Are we still walking in our
own ways? Are we still trying to carve out a space in the jar or have
we found our way to the lily pad? Everything around us is changing so

quickly, but some of us have become so rooted in our thinking that we believe that the "old-time religion " is still good enough for us. If we are to be effective in the culture we now live in, then change is necessary. For example, the scripture gives us our functions, which don't change evangelism or discipleship. We express those functions in the type of musical instruments we use which must change if we're to influence the cultural groups around us. If we're not creative, we wind up freezing in time, locking into 1955 forms.

The epistle of James 1: 22-25 says; "But be ye doers of the word, and not hearers only, deceiving your own selves. For if any be a hearer of the word, and not a doer, he is like unto a man beholding his natural face in

Marshall Shelley, vol. 2, Empowering Your Church Through Creativity and Change : 30 Strategies to Transform Your

Ministry, 1st ed., Library of Christian leadership (Nashville, Tenn.: Moorings, 1995), 66.

a glass: [24]For he beholdeth himself, and goeth his way, and straightway forgetteth what manner of man he was. [25] But whoso looketh into the perfect law of liberty, and continueth therein, he being not a forgetful hearer, but a doer of the work, (This Man Shall Be Blessed) in his deed". It is not enough just to know the word of God. The problem is there is too many who know the word but few who are willing to walk in it. If we are to be blessed in all that we do, we must be doers of that word and not just hearers only. If we are to be the manifestation of Gods' glory here on earth, then we must be obedient to his will (meaning His Word) and walk in it. The Lord said in St John 15:7-8; "If ye abide in me, and my Words abide in you, ye shall ask what ye will, and it shall be done unto you. Herein is my Father glorified, that ye bear much fruit; so shall ye be my disciples". We are to live our lives daily as instruments showing how to walk and how not to walk with a holy (set apart from sin) God.

It's important for us to get the word in us, but if we are to be blessed, we must <u>PERFORM</u> it. The psalmist said in Psalms 119: 105-106:"Thy word is a lamp unto my feet, and a light unto my path. 106 says: I have sworn, and I will perform it, that I will keep thy righteous judgments.

CHAPTER FOUR

WHAT DOES IT MEAN TO WALK AFTER

THE SPIRIT?

Walking in the spirit is the theme that is often referred to by the Apostle Paul in the epistles. The question of what it means to walk in the spirit must be examined in light of who and what the spirit is. Acts 1:8 says, "But ye shall receive power, after that the Holy Ghost is come upon you: and ye shall be witnesses unto me both in Jerusalem, and in all Judaea, and in Samaria, and unto the uttermost part of the earth. Luke 21:31-32; "And the Lord said, Simon, Simon, behold, Satan hath desired to have you, that he may sift you as wheat: [32] But I have prayed for thee, that thy faith fail not: and when thou art converted, strengthen thy brethren". These men were disciples who walked with Christ for three long years. They ate with him, laugh with him quite possibly cried with him, and done all those things that close friends do together. Although they were believers, they did not have what it took to do or be what they were called to be. There was something else they needed to be affective witnesses of Christ Jesus. They needed Power. All these men knew the Lord and had personally walked with him, talked

7The King James Version; 1611 Authorized Version. Lk. 21:31,32.

with him, ate with him, and witnessed the awesome miracles he had performed, and yet, they did not have what it took to get the job done. Take Peter for instance, not only do we need this power to live right, but for Christian service as well because service is a part of Christian living. Jesus said, "ye shall receive power AFTER that the Holy Ghost is come upon you". Seems to me these disciples could not be affective witnesses for Christ until after the Holy Ghost (power) would come upon them. If it was true for them, then it should be true for us as well? It is good to learn the Word, to study to show ourselves approved unto God, to get the Word in us because it is the Word of God that gives us the life of God, and it is the Spirit of God that gives us the power of God. Two, I John 1:5 says, "the Father, the Word, and the Holy Ghost: and these three are one". St. John 6:63 Jesus says, "It is the spirit that quickeneth; the flesh profiteth nothing: the words that I speak unto you, they are spirit, and they are life". Here we focus not only on what He (the spirit) does but what He (the spirit) is. Jesus himself said "it is the spirit that quickeneth". The word quickeneth, translated from the Greek text means to (give life; to make alive), and so the thought here is that it is the spirit that gives life or, it is the spirit that makes alive. Then he said" The words that I speak unto you, they are spirit and they are life". The idea we get from this statement is "the WORD that I speak to you they are SPIRIT" they are life", (they make alive, or they give life). So, to walk in the spirit is to walk in the word or what the word of God says concerning us and His will. The spirit and the word are one, different administrations, but one and the same. I John 5 say, "For there are three that bear record in heaven, the Father, the Word, and the Holy Ghost: <u>and these are one</u>". Walking in the Spirit is not coming out of the body and transcending up into some spiritual realm where everyone floats around, flapping their arms and talking slowly. Walking in the spirit is essentially taking control of the unhealthy desires of the fleshly man and bringing him under subjection and the obedience of the Word of God. The problem is, that there is this spiritual battle going on between the outer and the inner man within us; one against the other for control over our destinies.

CHAPTER FIVE

WHAT DOES IT MEAN TO WALK AFTER THE FLESH?

It is very important for believers to realize who they are. If we don't understand who we are in Christ Jesus, then we can do no spiritual exploits for the Lord. Too often we try to do the work of the Lord in the flesh and we're not getting the job done. The objective here is to help us understand who we are and what it means to walk after the flesh. Let us go to the beginning. Genesis 1: 26a, "And God said, Let us make man in our image, after our likeness: When God created man he created him in his image and after his likeness. "The image and likeness of God (1:26—27) is most immediately linked to humanity's power to rule over creation (1:26) and to reflect the <u>nature</u> and <u>graces</u> of male and female gender. Human gender reflects God's infinitely deep character as the potent Creator and the perfectly wise, loving, and nurturing Person[1](1:27). Jesus said in John 4:24, "God is a Spirit: and they that worship him must worship him in spirit and in truth". This should indicate that neither His image nor character is rooted in male or female gender but as spiritual. And those that relate to him must do so in spirit and in truth. Jesus discloses the fact that "God is a Spirit" and they that worship him must worship him in spirit and truth. If God is a Spirit, and we are created in his image, then we are spirit beings as well. Let us examine this a bit <u>closer</u>. Not only were we created in his image, but also in his likeness.

1 Robert B. Hughes and J. Carl Laney, Tyndale Concise Bible Commentary, Rev. Ed. of: New Bible Companion. 1990.;

Includes Index., The Tyndale reference library (Wheaton, Ill.: Tyndale House Publishers, 2001), 10.

The word "Spirit" that Jesus spoke of is translated from the Greek text as pneuma/ pnyoo-mah, meaning an animated or vital principal held to give life to physical organisms/ breath of nostruls of mouth/ a malevolent being that is bodiless but can become visible. A spirit is an entity that exist and is just as real as you and I, but bodiless. This is a far cry from the cartoon character Casper the friendly ghost. Spirits are not white blobs with eyes, noses and mouths that float around trying to scare folks to death. They are bodiless entities that do not have bodies as we do but have been known to appear in human or bodily forms. One such case mentioned in the scripture is when Saul, king of Israel disguised himself to go see the witch at Ender to bring up the spirit of Samuel the prophet from the dead for counsel, I Samuel 28: 10-25. So, we discover spirits do indeed exist on another plane that most of us are totally unaware of. My intention here is not to prove that spirits exist, but to simply identify and to point out the differences between the spirit and the flesh. The body is a part of our existence. The Godhead (1: divine nature or essence of God); (2: the nature of God esp. as existing in three persons) is the nature of God existing in three persons, (father, son and Holy Ghost), His Divine nature or essence. Man, moreover, is made up of three parts as well, body soul and spirit. The part that is more like God is our spirit (the heart of man). Once the spirit is separated from the body (dust) and the soul, it will inevitably return to God: Ecclesiastes 12:4-7. On the contrary the flesh (body, dust), not divine in nature but is made from the dust of the ground; Genesis 2:6-7, "But there went up a mist from the earth, and watered the whole face of the ground. [7] And the LORD God formed man of the dust of the ground and breathed into his nostrils the breath of life; and man became a living soul". In Genesis 3:19 God said, "In the sweat of thy face shalt thou eat bread, till thou return unto the ground; for out of it wast thou taken: for dust thou art, and unto dust shalt thou return. The body (flesh) has a nature of its own just as the spirit has a nature of its own. While the spirit is subject to the law of God, the body (the flesh) is not; Romans 8:5-7 says;" For they that are after the flesh do mind the things of the flesh; but they that are after the Spirit the things of the Spirit. 6 -For to be carnally minded is death; but to be spiritually minded is life and peace. 7 Because the carnal mind is enmity against God: for it is not subject to the law of God, neither indeed can be". The word flesh and carnal are used interchangeably and are synonymous with the other. So, they that are after the flesh are the same as those who are carnal minded. Galatians 5: 16-18 says; "This I say then, walk in the Spirit, and ye shall not fulfil the lust of the flesh. [17] For the flesh lusteth against the Spirit, and the Spirit against the flesh: and these are contrary the one to the other: so that ye cannot do the things that ye would. [18] But if ye be led of the Spirit, ye are not under the law ". By continually depending upon and yielding to God, the believer can live under the power of the Holy Spirit and does not need to carry out the desires that seek to hold control over his physical body the sinful nature. Paul recognized that there was a continual war going on between the physical flesh and the Holy Spirit to inspire the life of a believer (5:17). In light of the Galatians' conflict over keeping the law, Paul was saying that walking by the Spirit is living by grace, not by the keeping of the law. It is living because of God's grace, not in order to gain it. What are some of the attributes of the flesh? Verse 19 says; "Now the works of the flesh are manifest, which are these; Adultery, fornication, uncleanness, lasciviousness, 20 Idolatry, witchcraft, hatred, variance, emulations, wrath, strife, seditions, heresies, 21 Envyings, murders, drunkenness, revellings, and such like: of the which I tell you before, as I have also told you in time past, that they which do such things shall not inherit the kingdom of God". The objective here is for us to realize who we really are and begin to live and act according to our divine nature. The heart of man is his spirit, the very essence of his being. The spirit of man is who we really are. That blood-pumping organ that is inside the chest of the body is just what it is, an organ of the body (The Flesh), and is called the heart. Just as this organ is essential for delivering the life-giving blood to the body, it is the Holy Ghost (Spirit of God) that is essential for delivering the life-giving power of God to us (the spirit of man). This is why when God looks on man, he looks on the inward parts, (the heart the spirit), because he's looking at man as he really is. Once we understand who we really are, then we can do all things through

Christ who strengthens us". We are spiritual beings and God has placed in us his divine nature. The question is, will we begin to live in that divine nature, or will we continue to live, (Walk in), or after the flesh, that carnal nature? Let us focus on some of the attributes of the flesh, (sight, hearing, feelings, emotions, etc.). The disciple Thomas, called Didamus, was not with the other disciples when Jesus appeared to them in the house. When he finally joined them, something happened. Let us examine St. John 20: 24-25; "But Thomas, one of the twelve, called Didymus, was not with them when Jesus came. [25] The other disciples therefore said unto him, we have seen the Lord. But he said unto them, Except I shall see in his hands the print of the nails and put my finger into the print of the nails, and thrust my hand into his side, I will not believe". Note, except I shall- SEE-I will not believe". Now how many of us have at one time or another said those very same words, even concerning spiritual things, "l will not believe it until I see it" is the cliché that has stunted our spiritual growth and robbed us of the blessings that God had intended for our lives. Let us also examine the words of Jesus concerning this carnal attitude in verses 26-30. "And after eight days again his disciples were within, and Thomas, then came Jesus, the doors being shut, and stood in the midst, and said, Peace be unto you. Then saith he to Thomas, reach hither thy finger, and behold my hands; and reach hither thy hand, and thrust it into my side: and be not, faithless, but believing. 28 And Thomas answered and said unto him, My Lord and my God. [29] Jesus saith unto him, Thomas, because thou hast SEEN me, thou hast believed: blessed" are they, that have not seen and yet have believed. One of the main reasons we are not blessed in what we do is because of the Thomas syndrome. We have to see it to believe it. Jesus said, "BLESSED are they That have not seen, and yet believe". My argument is, if we are to live this life and live it more abundantly, then we are going to have to learn to walk by faith and not by sight. The confession "My Lord and my God" vs (28) is remarkable for its theological grasp. Whether or not Thomas fully understood his own words, this unmistakably high concept of the divine nature provides a fitting conclusion to John's record of the path of faith. Nevertheless, the weakness of Thomas' confession was that it depended on sight. Jesus needed to make an important point here by mentioning the greater blessedness of those who believe without seeing, which applies to all Christian believers ever since the time of Jesus. We depend upon secure evidence (Scripture, the witness of the church through the ages, our own experiences) but not on actually seeing Jesus. Too many of us are trying to walk by sight, rather than by faith.

As I have mentioned, sight is one of the attributes of the flesh, and if we walk in the flesh we shall die. Time after time we have been faced with situations in our lives when things were not looking good. Some of us are facing difficult situations now in our lives. And it's not looking good at all. Let me encourage you in the word of God. It is not always how it looks or how it sounds that will determine the outcome but let me remind you that it is what God says about the situation that determines the outcome. If we trust him and take him at his word regardless of what it looks, sounds, or feels like, then we will be blessed and have good success. "Blessed are they that have not seen, and yet have believed. Il Corinthians. 5:7 (For we walk by faith, not by sight:). Remember, sight is an attribute of the flesh. Let us talk about feelings. Because of our feelings, God have been robbed of the praises in which he inhabits of the saints. It is not that we intentionally do this, but because of either tradition or a lack of teaching in the local churches. When we come into the presence of other believers, habitually we might say, Praise the Lord. From the pulpit the preacher himself would say to the congregation," well praise the Lord saints", and in return we will automatically repeat the phrase, "Well praise the Lord". In this entire process, no one has actually praised the Lord. Like a parrot we will repeat what we heard: "Praise the Lord, praise the Lord", and God has not been praised yet. Yet we all know that the highest praise we can give God is hallelujah, but when we are asked to praise the Lord we say, "praise the Lord". Through this exchange, God has yet to be praised. When someone say to you from now on, Praise the Lord, then praise him by saying Hallelujah. Then there are those who come to church week after week, take the same old seat in the church, sit around until the service is over, and not once, given God the praise. They get upset when someone sitting close would stand and openly give God his praises. We can guess, but only God knows what insults they are hurling through their minds. One thing I know for sure concerning praises, it is commanded that we come into the house of the Lord with praises. Psalms 100: 4 "Enter into his gates with thanksgiving, and into his courts with praise: be thankful unto him and bless his name". So many of us are leaving home with all the burdens from the week before, worried, sick and tired, angry, frustrated and downright disgusted. The way we are feeling and the things we are going through seem to dictate our relationship with God. While it is true that sometimes it may feel that God is nowhere near or that he has forgotten us when He was passing out blessings, it is important for us to realize that our relationship with God has nothing to do with the way we feel or what we think. It has everything to do with what the word of God has to say about the situation, and what we believe. The position to take here is when we come into the sanctuary with all these negatives in our hearts and minds, we sit hoping for something to happen from the outside, not realizing that the process of worship, peace and deliverance begins within us. When we come in, why not enter his gates with thanksgiving and into his courts with praise? The process begins with us, and it ends with God doing his part. The next time you are in a worship service, and you just don't feel like praising God, you don' feel like raising your hands to give Him what is due, do it anyway, "draw night to God and he will draw nigh to you " James 4:8. There certainly are life-changing experiences that we have yet to tap into. By no means am I saying it will be easy but what I am saying is I know we can do it, "For we can do all things through Christ which strengthens us " Philipians 4:13. God is indeed a just God that would never tell us to do something he knows we cannot do. What we must do is trust him and try him. God is faithful, I know, because I tried him for myself and I can say, truly, God is faithful. For far too long we have settled for and have operated in the lower nature(flesh) trying to do the work God has called us to do. Then we ask ourselves the question, why is this so difficult? The answer is that we have been trying to do spiritual work with the flesh and with the carnal mind and weak faith not trusting that God will do what he says He will do. The fleshly man will only do so much and go so far as we well know. The second things don't look good, smell good, sound good, or more importantly feel good, then we lose interest and begin to support the fleshly carnal minded part of our nature, where there's no profit or glory, from that point on things began to get difficult. The inward battle begins to rage, and the downside to it is, the one you've been feeding and walking with the longest will be the strongest. Do the math. As the apostle Paul noted in Romans 8:12-14, "[12]Therefore, brethren, we are debtors, not to the flesh, to live after the flesh. [13] For if ye live after the flesh, ye shall die: but if ye through the Spirit do mortify or (Crucify) the deeds of the body, ye shall live. [14]

10 The King James Version of the bible. The Authorized 1611 Version. James 4:8.

For ye have not received the spirit of bondage again to fear; but ye have received the Spirit of adoption, whereby we cry, Abba, Father". We have what it takes to be victorious and conquerors of the flesh. What we must do is believe what God has said concerning us, It Must Be So. No longer do we have to speculate, wondering if God will do what he said he would do. Let me make the point that God has done all he is going to do concerning his plan for our salvation, deliverance, and victory. The rest is up to us. My concern is that not all of us are willing to make the necessary sacrifices to make this a reality for our own lives. In the flesh, we don't have a chance, but through Christ, we can do all things. The first step is ours. Let us rise up out of this carnal-minded, flesh-driven nature and begin walking with the mind of Christ and the Spirit of God. Things may look impossible but remember we serve the God that specializes in impossibilities. Sometimes the way does seem dark, but remember, His word is a lamp unto our feet, and a light unto our path. Jesus is the light of the world. Friends may forsake us, but we have a friend who sticks closer to us than a brother; He will never leave nor forsake us. We have this heritage that gives us the right to God's bosom and how have we responded to this wonderful unmatchable gift? Have we given this any kind of real consideration as to what God has already done for us? It can be mind-boggling just to try and conceive just who and what God is. The creator of the very foundations of the universe and for some reason, we can't seem to take Him at His word. He is the Word. HE-IS- GOD!

CHAPTER SIX
STANDING ON THE WORD
OF GOD

"Standing on the word of God" can be a cliché sometimes used to emphasize the importance of obeying or performing the word of God, no matter the cost. What does it mean to stand on the word of God?

Proverb 3:5-7. "⁵Trust in the LORD with all thine heart; and lean not unto thine own understanding. ⁶In all thy ways acknowledge him, and he shall direct thy paths. ⁷Be not wise in thine own eyes: fear the LORD and depart from evil". Standing on the Word of God has often been used as the criteria for entering the kingdom of God. This has been done without regard as to whether it is understood by the believer or not. It is wise to know what the word says, but it is better if we have an understanding also. This brings us to our first question, "What does it mean to stand on the word of God"? Somewhat analytical, my first objective was to see what the bible has to say about the problem and secondly, how does this work. Consequently, this brings me to the Word of God, "Trust in the Lord with all thine heart", the bible says, and "lean not to thine own understanding". It is at this point in our journey where many of us fail to make the grade. If I am not to apply my own understanding to a given situation; then who's understanding or whose methods should I use to solve the problems that life forces me to confront? After all, we have made all the decisions that have gotten us where we are today. Considering all this, commonsense forces me to see just where I really am, and moreover, how I got here in the first place.

So how did we get here? Well, we have a way of sizing up a situation, measuring the pros and cons, and deciding and making the decisions that best suit our purpose or need at the time. If it's a delicate situation, and a lot is riding on the decisions we make, we dare not trust anyone else to such a task but ourselves. We don't trust anyone, and we tend to lean to our own understanding and ours alone. In light of all this, we now realize how we got where we are. So, what do we do about the fine mess we have gotten ourselves into? How do we escape this cycle of madness? This is not really going up or down, or around and around in circles, but never really going anywhere. Through this cloudy maze of darkness, the Word of God brings us light, and gives us hope, but most of all, the courage to say I am better, I can do better, and I will be better. We need to trust God and more importantly, take him at his word. The fact that God has more confidence in us than we have in ourselves should inspire us to examine more closely our own true God-given abilities. If He tells us to do something, it's obvious He knows we can do it.

<u>Now think about that for a moment.</u> We, we are the ones having problems believing what God already knows, or what He says concerning us. Personally, I believe we serve a loving and just God. And I know He would never tell me to do something He knew I couldn't do. I'm inclined to believe that if God said it, then it is possible and it must be so. With all these things to take into account, the question that comes to mind that must be answered is; <u>How does one stand on the word of God ?</u>

Matt. 14:25-29; The Bible said. "And in the fourth watch of the night Jesus went unto them, walking on the sea. [26] And when the disciples saw him walking on the sea, they were troubled, saying, "it is a spirit"; and they cried out for fear. [27] But straightway Jesus spake unto them, saying, Be of good cheer; it is I; be not afraid.[28] And Peter answered him and said, Lord, if it be thou, bid me come unto thee on the water. [29] And He said, Come. And when Peter was come down out of the ship, he walked on the water, to go to Jesus".

Now, for the purpose of illustration, let me reiterate. After sending his disciples to the other side of the lake, something happened while they were in the midst of this lake. A storm arose and the boat they were in was being hammered by the stormy winds, no doubt the rains, the thunder, and the lightning raged. And they found themselves in the midst of a very large and terrible storm. To the disciples, it may have looked like they were going to sink, but then something strange happened. They looked and saw what seemed to be a spirit coming toward them, walking on the water. Troubled by what they saw, the bible says they became afraid. Then, they realized it was Jesus coming to them walking on the water. The first words Jesus spoke to Peter and the rest of the disciples were "Fear Not". Jesus immediately, recognized there was a problem, one that had to be dealt with before Peter could obey the spiritual command that was about to be given to him by Jesus. You see, Fear paralyzes, and will destroy and leave a strong man weak, a rich man poor and destitute, a wise man cursed with the knowledge and understanding but without the courage to perform and dawn the anointed mantle of sonship. Fear is a spirit, a spirit with the ability to kill, steal, and destroy. Fear is the thief of all times, but Jesus gave Peter something to overcome this killer. He gave him the word, His Word, and it only took one word, and that word was "COME". The word of God tells us that Peter took Christ at his word and stood on that word. Regardless of how bad the situation looked, or how treacherous the winds were, or how much the rains came down, with the lightning flashing and the thunder roaring, the bible said that Peter, climbed down out of that boat, and <u>WALKED</u>, on the water to go to Jesus. Matt. 14:29: And he said, "<u>COME</u>". And when Peter was come down out of the ship, he walked on the water to go to Jesus. Peter made a conscious decision not to walk by sight, nor by what he saw, but by faith, he acted, or performed what the word of God said, "COME". So, we see, standing on the word of God means to do, to perform what God has commanded. Take him at his word, and as the late Kenneth Hagan Sr. would say "trust the fact that when we do it the bible way, we'll get bible results".

CHAPTER SEVEN
HINDRANCES TO CHRISTIAN PROGRSS

We have spoken a lot about the Power for Christian Living but what about those things that would keep us from practicing what we know. How do we do what we know? First, let us identify the problems and then use what we know to overcome or solve them. Let us remember not to deviate from the Word of God for the answers. If we are to be successful with spiritual things, we must draw from our spiritual source, the Word.

Hosea 4:6 says, " [2]My people are destroyed for lack of knowledge: because thou hast rejected knowledge, I will also reject thee that thou shalt be no priest to me: seeing thou hast forgotten the law of thy God, I will also forget thy children". In the first clause of this scripture God said that ("His" people") were destroyed for lack of knowledge". In the world that we live in, it said that knowledge is power. According to the first clause of this scripture the same seems to hold true spiritually. As a prior military man, I'm convinced that until you learn and know your enemy, and their methods of operation, there is not much chance of any kind of victory over your them. Many wars have been lost throughout history because leaders failed to know their enemies. The bible has been read from Genesis to Revelations, God from the beginning to the end, the wonderful stories of the great things He done through His people and others who would dare to love and take Him at his word.

---

2 The King James Version of the Bible. The Authorized Version Of the KJV. Hosea 4:6.

Mighty acts were done concerning things that seemed impossible or unreal. We fail to see that the enemy is there too, lurking in the background and sometimes in the forefront. All those wonderful stories of the great things God did through His people and others who would dare to love and take Him at his word. The question is: What have we learned about how the devil operates? Have we learned anything about how he deceives in order to keep us in darkness?

"My people are destroyed for lack of knowledge". "In St. John 10: 10 Jesus said,"The thief cometh not, but for to steal, and to kill and to destroy, I am come that they might have life and that they might have it more abundantly". The enemy's method of operation according to Jesus is that he is a thief. When someone steals something, it is usually something of value. One thing to realize is that the thief we are referring is not a man, though he uses men and women to do his bidding. He's waged an all-out spiritual warfare against God to steal the souls of men. And if he can keep man in darkness through the lack of the knowledge that God wants us to know then the battle is in his favor. What does he want to steal? The knowledge of God, the Word of God and once he is able to steal the word, or keep us ignorant of it, he is able to keep us in darkness. His next objective is to kill men in their ignorance that their souls would be lost and, in the process, destroy those lives caught in his snare. In all this chaos we find that there is hope. Jesus said "I come that they might have life and have it more abundantly. "The Lord came that we might have life and it more abundantly. It's sad to say that there are so many of us who have life but will never experience it more abundantly as He had intended. This is due in part to the fact that we have rejected the knowledge of God, and this comes with consequences. When it comes to doing His will, we reject the fact that we can do all things through Christ who gives us the strength to do so. When it comes to health, we reject the fact that with His stripes we were healed. We would rather see it or feel it before we will believe what He has already done. Thomas spent a lot of time with Jesus before the crucifixion but did not believe it when the disciples told him that they had seen the Lord after His resurrection. Thomas would not believe it until he saw it for himself. Again what is more interesting is what Jesus said to Thomas after He appeared to him: "Thomas, because thou hast seen me, thou hast believed: blessed are they that have not seen, and yet have believed. The lack of faith in the word of God and what the word says concerning us is a hindrance to our Christian progress. It denies us of the power which comes from the word, Powerf or Christian Living. Someone has said once that "what we don't know won't hurt us". Personally, I beg to differ. What we don't know could actually kill and destroy us. This is also one of the reasons we are not blessed in our press. We have to believe even before we see. If the word said it then it must be true. This can be a paradox because all of what we do, know, or have experienced have been based on what we've seen or felt. Regardless of what life presents or seems like, how it looks or how it feels, remember the word of the Apostle Paul in I Corinthians15:57, "But thanks be to God, which giveth us the victory through our Lord Jesus Christ". We have what it takes to believe without having to see. I John 5: 4, 5 declares that, " [4]For whatsoever is born of God overcometh the world: and this is the victory that overcometh the world, even our faith. Who is he that overcometh the world, but he that believeth that Jesus is the Son of God? We are guaranteed victory in this Christian walk if we apply the principles of the word. There are no limits to the spiritual exploits we are destined to achieve. Let us be reminded what the Apostle Paul said in Ephesians 6:16" Above all, taking the shield of faith, wherewith ye shall be able to quench all the fiery darts of the wicked". Paul said above ALL, take the shield of faith that you will be able to ward off the attacks of the devil. After enlisting in the US Army, I understood within myself that I was enlisting into the most powerful and respected armed forces in the world. I had no doubt that if I had to face any enemy on the globe, we would win that war. I had blind faith that I was on the winning team, even before we faced the enemy. I had my shield, and nothing could take it away. The first week I was issued my clothing. Obviously, I couldn't go into combat as a naked soldier. These clothing were made especially for the harsh elements I would have to endure out on the battlefield. I quickly realized that if I had not put on the correct clothing, I couldn't function as an effective soldier. Today, I find myself in a different army fighting a different enemy on an entirely different level of existence. Earlier, I mentioned that we are in a spiritual warfare and in spiritual warfare we cannot use carnal (natural) weapons against this enemy because he is a spiritual being who operates in the spiritual realm. I realized this time; I had enlisted in the most powerful army in the universe and to be victorious in this army would have to use the spiritual weapons that God gave us to be successful. First, I found that in this army there was something I had to put on and it had to be Christ Jesus. He would cover and help me to weather all I would have to go through. Romans 13: 14 the Apostle Paul says "But put ye on the Lord Jesus Christ and make no provision for the flesh to fulfill the lust thereof". Verse 17 says "And take the helmet of salvation, and the sword of the Spirit, which is the word of God. Let me elaborate a moment. The helmet of salvation and the sword of the Spirit each has a specific function. When I enlisted into the Army, the first week I was issued standard gear to be able to function as a soldier. Most of this gear was foreign to me and I had no idea of how to use most of it. Soon I began to receive the training I needed to become proficient and effective. Over and over, again and again, day in and day out we trained until we were able to use that gear in our sleep if we had to. I learned that a helmet is a very important piece of gear. It is not designed specifically to stop a bullet from penetrating the skull, but it may deflect one and will protect the skull and brain from shrapnel (pieces of flying metal from an explosion or fragmented bullet). You need a helmet in spiritual or carnal warfare but without it, you will surely pay the price, "And take the helmet of salvation". If we need a helmet in the natural army for warfare, should we not need a spiritual helmet in this spiritual warfare? What does a spiritual helmet protect? I'm confident that if a natural helmet will help protect the head from the onslaught of foreign objects, the spiritual helmet will help protect the mind from the onslaught of evil influences from the devil. If he can steal our minds, he can control our destiny. "Take the helmet of salvation and the sword of the Spirit". Why take the sword of the Spirit? The sword of the Spirit is the Word of God. To take the Sword of the Spirit is to take the POWER OF God, the enemy knows there is power in the Word of God. It was the word that quenched his attacks against Jesus in the wilderness. We see in

St. Matthew the 4th chapter verses 1-4, each time he came against Jesus, Jesus used the written word of God to defend himself. We see the Lord using the Sword of the Spirit to battle against a spiritual foe. He knew He could not use carnal weapons to fight against the devil, so he used what was appropriate, the sword of the Spirit. To use carnal weapons to battle against a spiritual enemy is a losing battle. The devil knows this and is one of the reasons he does so much to keep us from learning and knowing the word of God. Once we learn, and once we know, then we are well on our way to spiritual progress and success.